All rights reserved. No part of this publication may be reproduced, distributed, or transmitted in any form or by any means, including photocopying, recording, or other electronic or mechanical methods, without the prior written permission of the publisher, except in the case of brief quotations embodied in critical reviews and certain other noncommercial uses permitted by copyright law.

This book is a work of nonfiction. The views expressed are those of the author alone and should not be taken as expert instruction or commands. The publisher and author are not responsible for the use of any content herein, and the responsibility for any action taken based on this book lies solely with the reader.

Printed in the United States of America

TAKING THIS WALK WITHOUT YOU

INSPIRED BY:
HOLY SPIRIT

AUTHORED BY;
SYMONE ANDERSON

EDITED BY:
SELENA JACKSON

CONTENTS

FOREWARD

DEDICATION

PREFACE

PART I

LETTING GO OF YOUR HAND

1 Fear

2 Disbelief

PART II

UNPACKING THIS PAIN ALONE

3 Sadness

4 With These Tears

5 Anger

6 Depression

CONTENTS

PART III
ACQIESCENCE IN SEPARATION

7 Surrender

8 At His Feet

9 Ontogeny

PART IV
FREEDOM THROUGH GOD'S REVELATION

10 Love

11 A Mother's Love

AFTERWORD

FOREWARD

IN A WORLD OFTEN INTENT ON GLOSSING OVER PAIN

with the superficial distractions of modern life all around us, I find a voice within that insists on speaking truth to the aching heart. This book is that voice—a powerful testament to my raw, unfiltered journey through grief, revealing the complexity of human emotions and spiritual resilience.

In these pages, I present a tapestry woven from threads of sorrow, faith, and unshakable hope. Through a literary grace that embodies profound vulnerability, I invite you into the crucible of my grief. My words don't merely describe suffering; they articulate it with such vividness and honesty that I hope you, too, will confront your own hidden wounds.

Grief, in its most elemental form, is an intense experience that tests the very core of our faith. For many, it can feel as though the connection to God is severed—a cruel irony in moments when His presence is most needed. Yet, in those moments of strained connection, I find and reveal an undeniable truth: our bond with God may stretch and strain, but it is never truly broken. The God who stands with us in our joy does not retreat in our sorrow.

FOREWARD

INSTEAD, HE DRAWS NEARER, OFFERING HIS UNFAILING LOVE AS A BALM FOR OUR ACHING SOULS.

Through my evocative, poetic prose, this book becomes a sanctuary where grief and grace intersect. It is a privilege for me to share such an intimate dance between pain and divine comfort. My reflections are not just personal; they resonate with an infallible truth—that the depth of our suffering is met with the depth of God's love. My journey underscores a vital lesson: to feel deeply is not a weakness, but a profound testament to our humanity and to the sustaining presence of God.

As you embark on this journey through grief with me, I hope you find solace in my words and strength in my testimony. May my insights illuminate the path through your own sorrows and remind you of the enduring, unbreakable connection we share with God. In the embrace of these pages, may you discover that even in our darkest moments, we are held close by a God whose unconditional love never fails.

THIS LITERARY WORK IS

DEDICATED TO

the reader of this book, as you travail along these pages that house deep reflections poured and spilling out from my heart to yours.

My hope for you, as each word is read and received that you most importantly understand your emotional stance through your journey.

May this book allow you to feel safe enough, to become undone within the gentle embrace of God's unconditional love.

To arrive at the place where you accept the beautiful gift that you are undeniably, infallibly, unequivocally seen, felt and held intimately by God.

PREFACE

AS I STOOD IN THE ROOM

where my mother laid, our eyes touched each other while a warm embrace of her hand wiped my tears away. There we were trapped in this moment of deep love, truth, and heartache. I witnessed her last breath, fleeting and shallow. As she took one last look at me, I swept in close to her ear speaking courageously while fighting the painful ripping of my heart and told her gently, "Thank you for being such an amazing woman and mother to me." A bold stillness overcame the sheer heartbreak in my voice and I said, "Run to Jesus mom, I love you." As my spine began to support me to move back into an upright position coming up from her ear, I retreated my arms from around the canvas of life that was once her. As I began to move further away, I caressed her fingertips. It was at this very moment, as I stared into her eyes that once encased strength and laughter but now a beautiful void that I knew it was the beginning of taking this walk without her.

We must not get tired of doing good. We will receive our harvest of eternal life at the right time. We must not give up.

Galatians 6:9 ERV Translation

"The journey is not influenced by the road ahead
but determined by the footsteps already taken."
-Symone Anderson

PART I

LETTING GO OF YOUR HAND

PART 1 : CHAPTER 1
FEAR

Coming into agreement with trepidation was never a part of my plans when caring for my mother. It always seemed to be leering over my shoulder as a constant reminder that at any moment, at any place, my mother could die and I would not be there. As I worked long days filled with meetings, trainings, and cases, I became accustomed to the fear I carried with me throughout my day. Combating my fear, which was constantly at war with my faith, was taxing. While I was thriving in my flesh, I was being tortured in my spirit. I found myself holding onto the familiarity of my control while desiring reckless abandonment of the comfort that my fear provided.

The imagery of a body emptied and barren without breath, a body split along the natural line where spirit and flesh once collided in my mind took residence within my heart. It caused me to frantically pour from my lips the deep desperation to have my emotions validated within this devastating experience. Many days I stayed in my office physically paralyzed as the emotional cycles kept me bound. I realized that my strength alone could not free me. The confession of losing my mother was not easy, especially to God. While He already knew what had me bound, I contended with the idea that I could achieve freedom on my own. Losing the control I never really had, which was birthed in a void inside of me, served as a meeting spot for my fear and anxiety to congregate.

As I surrendered to God and approached Him within my emptiness, He gave me peace. He gave me an infilling of renewed hope and faith. No longer restrained as a prisoner within the cerebral cemetery of the foreshadowing tenebrous possibilities and desecrated thoughts of a final goodbye being taken away from me.

*Do not fear (anything),
for I am with you; Do not
be afraid, for I am your
God.
I will strengthen you, be
assured I will help you; I
will certainly take hold of
you with my righteous
hand (a hand of justice, of
power, of victory, of
salvation).*

*Isaiah 41:10 AMP
Translation*

PART 1 : CHAPTER 1

FEAR

Dear God,

As I carry and lay this at your feet, I find myself consumed by the darkness that surrounds me. This burden I carry, a weapon that I did not intend to accompany me, has found a way to make itself the place in which my thoughts have chosen to exist. The intangible illusions trapped in my eyes and enclosed in my heart of my mother dying, as time runs away from me, seems like a reality that I am endowed to accept from the enemy. As days carry on, Lord, I find myself lost and arriving at the destinations of fear and confusion. Jesus, bring me your peace, the peace that surpasses all understanding; pour without end, Jesus, into the empty and deserted places in my heart.

Due to the treacherous attacks from the enemy, I began to believe that the only place I could operate from was located between my withering faith and the false confidence of control I applied to the fear consuming me. With the sleepless nights, tumbling in and out of your word, God I lay here spread thin - alternating between my control and your conviction. God, I know this is not how you envisioned me to live, to press forward with anxiety and disdain encompassing my heart.

Quicken to the portions of my soul that have been robbed of faith to defeat the enemy. God help me to be placed in the fullness of your armour to walk in undeniable authority. Father, who could have prepared me for such a battle as this other than you? As the days draw near and the time with my mother encloses, I request your strength to pursue each moment with your unwavering power and confidence.

Amen

PART 1 : CHAPTER 2
DISBELIEF

Sitting in the room across from an empty vessel was not easy for me. To witness God ushering my mother from glory to glory was a miracle that I will never forget. No one explained to me the depths that are involved when caregiving for someone, especially someone you love. There have been times when I have witnessed God's unfailing love and grace covering me through every moment that encompassed bathing, clothing, and feeding my mother. While some days were harder than others, Jesus held my hand through it all.

There were many nights I stayed in my car after arriving in the parking lot of my apartment to just sit in the stillness and silence at the end of my day. These were the moments I felt safe enough to be vulnerable with Jesus about the whirling emotions that accompanied me every day. To lay down the stress and impending expectations of others while releasing myself of the capacities I had become conditioned to fill. It all seemed to fall off my shoulders with every wailing cry and moan that persisted as each tear fell.

These were the moments I felt the constant outpouring of Jesus's love for me. Quite frankly...it was more than I had felt in a long time. I would show him the areas of my heart where I began to bleed out and would confess to Him my desperation to be filled with his strength to get through, just one more day. One more hour. One more minute. While existing in the duplicity of my doubt and faith, I felt God's presence closer to me than I realized.

Immediately the father of the boy cried out (with a desperate, piercing cry), saying, "I do believe; help (me overcome) my unbelief."

Mark 9:24 AMP Translation

PART 1 : CHAPTER 2

DISBELIEF

Dear God,

This moment for me is beyond what I can handle, seeing life leave someone I love in the last fleeting moments I had with her. Seeing her speak these final words, leaving behind a sweet gesture of a bewildering goodbye, and gifting me a lasting glance of love and deep reflection that ushered her into a place I could not go. As I sit here with my head sunken into my hands, the hands that once held life are seemingly struggling to console me. God, looking up seems so taxing with my eyes full of tears, masking my emotions that are falling down my face as I have no courage to speak of them. Jesus, you know every thought and feeling I am having, and you understand the strife that accompanies releasing a loved one from sickness and pain.

It feels like all parts of my body have begun to shut down with the numbness invading my heart. As memories begin to invade my mind and attempt to soften the attack of death, I fear this will not be enough to pacify the impending pain and heartache I am in. Lord, my heart is bleeding. With each new crack that is made, it is becoming harder to salvage the pieces as they fall away. The silence in this room is a loud and demanding clash of me pushing against my desires to break open and release, to pull apart the hazy thickness, to welcome the pace of solitude in this new wilderness. Be my guide God as I walk along this shaken foundation alone.

Bring me back to you, lead me to a place of understanding what I am going through.

Amen

PART II

UNPACKING THIS PAIN ALONE

"Our identity is not the product of the suffering we endure but through the expression of our faith to pursue life despite of it."
-Symone Anderson

PART 2 : CHAPTER 3
SADNESS

Within the night, I am ejected from temporary rest. I lean forward to become upright, sitting on the edge of my bed tarrying through the hallways of my mind trying to find a safe place to resign the macerated pieces of my heart. How have I found comfort wrapped in a foolish charade of home? With each breath I take, rage and acceptance dance among themselves trying to take the lead and guide how my body will respond to the cloak I wear that represents the involuntary loneliness your absence gifted me.

Oh, my contentious heart and mind vex me as I chase solace in the arms of my own deluded logic of what life has now become. It seems that normal modalities to achieve rest in my flesh and soul fail me in this very hour. It is here I shall live, in the barrows of the memories that keep you alive - a fading harlequin of youthful effigy wonderous and abounding in your eyes and smile. Oh infirmity! how you handled her with such sanguinary intrusiveness with your odious entrance, for she was not yours to have.

Mangled face, ablaze with the heat from my tears and eyes peeking through flesh abstaining from reaching out to you. Lord, here you are my fervid Savior. The one that sees me within the bosom of caliginosity. Your arms extended with loving extrication; I am found within the embrace of your grace and frabjous presence!

Where am I Lord that you do not see me? In my torment, despondency, and perdition you are there!

When the righteous cry [for help], the LORD hears And rescues them from all their distress and troubles. The LORD is near to the heartbroken And He saves those who are crushed in spirit (contrite in heart, truly sorry for their sin).

Psalms 34:17-18 AMP Translation

PART 2 : CHAPTER 3
SADNESS

Dear God,

Transpierced within me, is the twisting of vein and credulousness. Is this where true ascendancy is built between the divided cataclysmic void of a life untethered and hope? Growing here, among such thorns and vengeful gault, reaching for Sun, the Son, as I claw my way out of the masterful treachery that is revealed within the void of my eyes? Such joy, gleeful youth and bliss has run away, whisked into the arms of a deceptive, vehement lover. Are you searching for me Lord?

Do you bring such light, your incandescent righteousness my way, into the thick space of gelatinous shadows where flesh and weakness has led me? Oh, Father! Your light, a radiance only my spirit recognizes, a need my flesh longs to deny screaming in battle cries before war, charging into the fight. What makes a man fearsome and brave? Or a woman care for and nurture her child? For I am a babe again, in newness of breath and form. Where are you God, to pick me up? To nurse me? To hold me close to your bosom?

PART 2 : CHAPTER 3

SADNESS

Jesus, your word says that you are closer than a brother. Why I am left in the trenches of my soul, desperately clinging along the volatile anguish that cloaks me in the nights that tarry on longer than days? Ripping apart, tearing muscle and tissue within the caverns of my heart, I find you are here. Masterful carpenter, with needle and thread, sewing your soft words into the places where pain has chosen to reside. Dunamis power and presence are Yours to wear, displayed adornments of Your Holy glory.

Swaddled within the entrapment of death's mighty sting. Unraveling in between the veils of past and present, tasting the goodness of your mercy, chasing the glint of hope wrapped in the truth of your word. Will the vengeance of my sorrow ever end?

WITH THESE TEARS

WITH EYES THAT GREET YOURS

Meeting you here,
yet again with very little to give you
But with these tears, I long to share with you
Will you count it just enough?
* Or*
Cause me to sit alone
holding this sobering atonement for my sins?

Consorting with pain,
* broker a deal of temporary relief*
With the despair and anguish, a sinister family who
congregates to provide my broken comfort and false
sensibilities
Palms full of water escaping from the clefted vein of my
heart
Rushing into sunlight,
exhaling in your warmth, and soothing touch.

Calling out to me,
your Holy Spirit comforts me, a welcoming embrace into
your sovereign truth.
Falling from my face are the secrets my soul desperately
yearns to share with you,
Lord, please don't keep far from me.
With body afflicted and hungry flesh,
* still intact are the memories we have shared, to hold,*
forever, divinely cherished.

WITH THESE TEARS

WITH EYES THAT GREET YOURS

Meeting you here,
yet again with very little to give you
But with these tears, I long to share with you
Will you count it just enough?
 Or
Cause me to sit alone
 holding this sobering atonement for my sins?

Oh joy, reach out for me
within the deep blanket of night as I lay in the arms
of my doubt and shame.
Running, shuffling knees, weakness not far behind,
where the antipathy of this flesh collide into willful
submission by your Holy Spirit, where your glory reigns,
Lord your power prevails.

Discovering release,
within the endless bounty, illuminated landscape of your
love, it is here I shall remain, with these tears I shall use to
plant my life in you.

Branches birthed from you,
Tree of Life laboring fruit, a fragrant praise unto the
Lover of my soul, The Caretaker of
the fertile earth of my soul,
The interpreter of my tears.

With these tears, I shall run to you,
 Abba
Weeping and walking
into the arms of who my heart calls home.

PART 2 : CHAPTER 5
ANGER

Coiled within the grip of sour, venomous gall
feeling the rapturous discord of loneliness,
Who am I called to be here?

How can one persevere through
the ambiguous panorama of grief
 painting eyeless a life worth living?

My faith cascading,
canopied across ribboning skies
Hurling my last line of hope, cherishing the quaint possibility
There must be more surpassing this meridian of sinister
portion.

Through the perilous vacuity of deprivation
I rise beyond, to descry new revelation of
Your mercy, God!

Seeking me out, uplift me from the outspread mandible of
fiery castigation
and split me loose from the voracious jaws of
fleshly recompense
 to satisfy the score with the unyielding enemy,
lurking in obscurity, the grotesque knave,
the ultimate devourer.

PART 2 : CHAPTER 5
ANGER

Cradle me Oh God,
in the secret place, concealed away
in heavenly spiritual realms,
cloistered away from the treacherous beast.
 Lord the storm rages on within my soul,
waves bludgeoning against this boat,
Clashing of lightning, ringing of heavenly metal swords
ricochet off of the distant earth.
Cleanse me of this putrid stench of acridness and malicious
appetency.

Sitting quietly, with arms open
In the quietness of your garment
A conclave of unbuttoned vulnerability
Where you see me, God let your healing begin

While these chords traipse around me
You know the pain that is inside, longs to be unfettered.
Walking into faith,
unchained.

Wherefore is light given to him that is in misery, And life unto the bitter in soul; Who long for death, but it cometh not, And dig for it more than for hid treasures; Who rejoice exceedingly, And are glad, when they can find the grave? Why is light given to a man whose way is hid, And whom God hath hedged in? For my sighing cometh before I eat, And my groanings are poured out like water. For the thing which I fear cometh upon me, And that which I am afraid of cometh unto me.

Job 3:20-25 ASV Translation

PART 2 : CHAPTER 6
DEPRESSION

Sitting, waiting at the edge of existence while witnessing life and death swing in the bend of dimming light. Watching as it cascades across the sky cropped within the reflection of the mirror that I face. Arriving at this nebulous destination where time stands still with my hands losing its grasp and control. Life has become mundane and cold without warmth or joy barging in to rescue me from the snickering audience of my frayed emotions.

Burdened with heaviness and ladened with delayed joy.

Unresponsive to the light that surrounds me.

Swimming in deep turbulent waters unable to push through the ceiling of encapsulating blue speculum.

Imprisonment without freedom.

Life was distant . . . afar in reality . . . a reclusive dream. The journey through the despair is now so very close, suffocating the very space that my life disputatiously thrives in. Crippled by another manic episode of guilt and shame, it keeps me within the folds of bewilderment.

Within this cavernous vein.

PART 2 : CHAPTER 6
DEPRESSION

Arriving without concession or consent, walking into the
chasm of fractionalized delineation of who I am now.
Comforted by silence,
as the world turns the aperture inside of me yearns for a
touch,

a soft word to fill the void,
a lonely soul aching enfolded within the cerebral foundation
of my mind, a shadowed corner.

Having become hardened,
numbed to the core,
this is the result of me,
jaded and forlorn.

Untethered connection of moments that arrive greeted with
semblances of a fading smile to hide what is deeply shrouded
never to show, display, or explain.

Existing as a vacant enigma, a shell denuded of ardor and
strength to venture onward.
You call out to me in the gorge of my misery, Jesus.
In the quiet subjugation of grief. Your Holy Spirit, the
beautiful echo of your love, glorious expression of equanimity
and grace has found me. You are not confined to the
resplendent and majestic periphery of the heavens, for even
in my diminutive, truncated captivity, you surround me.

I waited patiently and expectantly for the LORD; And He inclined to me and heard my cry. He brought me up out of a horrible pit [of tumult and of destruction], out of the miry clay, And He set my feet upon a rock, steadying my footsteps and establishing my path.

Psalms 40:1-2 AMP

PART 2 : CHAPTER 6
DEPRESSION

Dear God,

Deliver me from this domain of exposure and fragility. I feel abandoned and forgotten within my affliction. Struggling to get out of my bed most days, subsiding with the denial of food and water I am clinging to the portions of my life that have run dry. Clasping the helm of your garment, Jesus I am unraveling, plummeting towards impending obliteration of the light within me. You are the only sure thing that can rescue me from myself. All my desire to live has become gargantuan without much reprieve in sight.

Can this body of clay, deep hues of rich Melanin earth be of good soil yet again? Father, hear my vociferations of desperation within this stockade of emotional calamity! For it is you who comes Lord to make wholeness from brokenness - produced by the residue caught in the storms of life. Do not leave me to meander through this place alone only to fall prey of my own deceitful heart of contorted truth. Keep me within your arms Abba safe from the thieves of joy awaiting to kill the little faith rooted deep inside. Coming to you Lord, exposed, indifferent and withdrawn from living, I am thirsty for your living water, to replenish the dry riverbeds of me.

Give me the courage Jesus to live beyond my pain. To be the recipient of your grace and mercy.

Through you Abba I shall live again.

Amen

*"As my flesh dies,
Yet my spirit dances
still for you, Lord."*
-Symone Anderson

PART III

ACQIESCENCE IN SEPARATION

PART 3 : CHAPTER 7

SURRENDER

The pulling away of pernicious comforts, the extraction of flesh from placid and safe places of vainglorious entrapments. Each layer being divested away in loving locution. I have never known such humbling disconcertion as this... The ripping away of pride, the cutting off of ego and self-idolism, the stripping away of sexual impurity, deviant behaviors, and the uprooting of hellish seeds planted within the fruitful soil of the rough curvature of mind and heart. Pulling until raw, excising the damage that lies within.

Who would clench so closely to such weapons of destruction to the soul? How could I have survived this long without your light inside of me Lord? I could not! For I have been your opponent in this fight; yet, it is my spirit that cries out to you from beyond the perpetual doublemindedness and impending loss of control that I fear. Should I give into you God? Who am I left to become if I do not find mollification within the pain accorded to me by those who are closest? With what I have, shall it be enough to use in the renewing of your creation? Should you have mercy on me, yet again?

PART 3 : CHAPTER 7
SURRENDER

Such are the labor pains of becoming.

Becoming more than the walking amalgamation of lies that outline the encamped citadel of my thoughts.

The imaginations of ambivalence and mendaciousness have conjured up such illusive storylines for my life to play out. Being deprived of light and air, gasping for that in which I have refused to acknowledge within myself for so long. Coming to the realization of my meek design that has been crafted by masterful skill and power.

Such raw nakedness taking shape and form; whom am I to be? Eyes closed, rushing into you, rapidly extricating all correlations of past exemplifications of self!

Arms outreached with water encasing the corners of my eyes. Oh, how I have longed to release from hands such weapons that have been my demise ABBA!

PART 3 : CHAPTER 7
SURRENDER

Dear God,

Living water traversing through me, heaviness disencumbered, such peace, heavenly sweetness trussed around me within just one look from you. Every version of myself is no comparison to who you have always known me to be. Oh faith, how you shall grow! Mightily and fiercely for all to see. Who knew, little mustard seed that you could be the heavenly manifestation of what God has created just for me? We shall dance, exuberantly, hand in hand, cheek to cheek underneath the rustling leaves of the mustard tree.

Such freedom in you Lord, is where I have longed to be, beyond the entombment of such sorrows onto the fullness of joy. Here I give you my heart, every beating vessel and vein. All circumference of my mind, every consuming word, dream and forethought magnanimous and minute. Every single finger, muscle, tendon and bone are all yours to do with what you will. Every breath, moment of eyesight, and sound of creation will witness your Dunamis power and healing embrace. For here I am, seen in the fullness of your being. Heard in silence and loud adjudication and lamentation. Here I am at the end of self-wisdom and empty philosophical madness.

Whom am I if not silhouetted by the truth kindled from your heart? What good is my life if it is not held within your hands? What worth does my name hold if it is not uttered from your lips? Here I am, a broken vacuous vessel waiting to be filled.

Here I am, Lord.

Lord, you look deep inside me, and you know all about me.
You know when I sit down, and you know when I get up.
Even when you are far away, you understand what I am thinking about.
You see me when I go out, and you see me when I stay at home.
You know everything that I do! Yes Lord, before I open my mouth to speak,
you know what I will say. You are all around me, in front of me and behind me.
You put your hand on me to help me. You know so much about me, it is wonderful.
I cannot understand it. My thoughts cannot reach as high as that!
7 Is there anywhere that I can go to run away from your Spirit?
Anywhere that I go, you are already there! If I go up to heaven,
you would be there. If I dig deep down into the ground to reach Sheol,
you would be there too.
If I fly away to where the sun rises in the east, or to the other side of the sea in the west,
you would be there. You would use your hand to lead me.
Your strong right hand would keep me safe. I might say, 'I will hide myself in the dark,
and the light round me will change into night.' But it is never too dark for you to see.
For you, the night has as much light as the day. Darkness and light are the same to you!
You made every part of me. You made me grow inside my mother before I was born.
I thank you for the wonderful way that you have made me. Everything that you do is wonderful!
I know it is true. While you caused me to grow in a secret place,
none of my body was hidden from you. You made me deep in the earth.
Your eyes watched me before I was born. Before I had seen the light of day,
you decided how many days I would live! You wrote it down in your book.
You have so many thoughts about me, God, that I cannot understand them all.
They are too many for me to count, more than the sand on the shore of the sea.
Even if I finished counting them, you would still be there!

Psalms 139: 1-18 EASY Translation

AT HIS FEET

FLESH AND SOUL DIVIDED

Pushing and pulling within me

Oh God, where your grace and mercy meet
Your love is abounding

Consuming fire and brazen strength and power
Refining

Broken heart shattered parts jagged and untamed
Within my pain I chose to remain

Your presence is beautiful abandoning all shame
Through your forgiveness came freedom
And redeemed is what you call me by name

"If you are too busy looking at the branches that God is cutting away, you run the risk of missing the opportunity to witness the birthing of good fruit."
   -Unknown

PART IV

FREEDOM THROUGH GOD'S REVELATION

PART 4 : CHAPTER 10

LOVE

It is the beauty glistening in moonlight. How the heavens awake at your presence, my beautiful King. The melody of creation swaying among the pantomime waters. Oh the joy my lover brings! As flowers bloom with every step you take towards me, as you are adored, oh Sweet Prince of Peace! My heart is yours to keep. Divinely cared for, exquisitely held and protected. Laying in peaceful tranquility within the caress of soft grass and warm soil.

Bubbling laughter as the Sun and Moon celebrate your crowning glory. All that once was, the combating anguish of death, the depletion of faith, the wrestling of worth and value are no more! The caress of your fingertips in mine, cupping the apple of my cheek, effortlessly washing away the sorrows that once stained my face.

No more shall I cleave to the deceitful impersonations of life fabricated among the tapestry of my past. For you alone quench the driest desert of my hungry soul; I shall thirst no more! In you my life has been resurrected into the full form of grace and mercy, clothed in crimson blood of beautiful sacrifice.

Hugging you, this closeness please never leave me, as the Morning dew passionately throws itself onto the stem of such youthful foliage and blushful paradise displayed covering the vast supple landscape of an ancient world.

ABBA!

PART 4 : CHAPTER 10
LOVE

Stay with me, Oh Lord, here within the meadows of melodic flowers in bloom. I am vein of your vein, blood rushing in, free flowing among arteries coiled masterfully! I have been resurrected, reborn into the newness of your smile, the gentle quiet of your eyes, gripping strength embroidered within the palms of your hands.

This cement prison, clanging chains singing along to the rhythm of my chiseled, stony heart. A familiar place I have never truly known, sought in the flaccid volumes of this sphere. Bring me closer to thee, yet one more time, to dwell in the pleasures of your heavenly delight. Let me stay cradled within your arms, once more.

Divine lover of my soul, oh how my heart quickens to be open within the core of your hands. Here with you, I feel seen. Here with you, I am all I need to be. Let us dance among the vast corridors of your splendiferous Kingdom of Heaven as she graces the Earth with her beauty and majesty.

I am found, rescued from the disdain of my humanity. When I am here; home is wherever you are. Oh what glory and favor have I found! Your words never fail. For they fiercely seek to return to you with deep devotion and endearing provocation.

I am truly his rose, the very theme of his song.
I'm overshadowed by his love, like a lily growing in the valley!
Yes, you are my darling companion. You stand out from all the rest.
For though the thorns surround you, you remain as pure as a lily, more than all others.
My beloved is to me the most fragrant apple tree—he stands above the sons of men.
Sitting under his grace-shadow, I blossom in his shade, enjoying the sweet taste of his pleasant, delicious fruit, resting with delight where his glory never fades.

Songs of Songs 2:1-3 TP Translation

A MOTHER'S LOVE

10 LITTLE HANDS 10 LITTLE FEET

How wonderful for us to meet
Healthy lungs displayed out loud
Oh, what joy my heart has found

Eyes capture, smiles in place
Button nose with warm embrace
How could I have ever thought life would be great,
without you here with me

Long nights and days filled with baby bottles
Sweeping through to a new tomorrow
Your lead I have begun to follow
As we dance this dance

Little clothes, little shoes
New outfits all the time
Taking you here and there
To show others how beautiful you are, so captivating, so
wonderful, so divine

Trying new things along the way
Witnessing the words, you will say
Seeing you laugh, smile and play
Makes life worth living

Seeing life through your eyes
Has me wondering all the time
How you will live as I, one day will not be beside you?

Just seeing you all grown up
And knowing how life has made you tough
Remember to not treat yourself as rough
As others have treated you

A MOTHER'S LOVE

SEASONS PASS ALONG

Winter, Spring, Summer
As Autumn leaves fall some may wonder
How can life fall away as leaves from a tree?

No matter the weather, the flowers that bloom or
the leaves that sail from tree to tree.
My love for you will never leave.

In the brazen sun we stand
Tightly woven hands
We both know in our hearts
This was God's plan

Seeing the world as brand new
From the moment I started loving you
Now as I know we have always been two
The time has come for there to be only one

As I walk through these gates with pain trailing behind
me
Leaning into God's glory – peace surrounding

Head held high, with tears flowing
Heart breaking, opening
Remember, what you are clothed in-
My love overflowing

Look outside and you will see
All the beauty that reminds you of me
Smile and dance for I am free

Being your mother was a blessing and you were my
greatest gift.

AFTERWORD

AS I PEN THESE FINAL THOUGHTS,

I find myself immersed in a deep reflection on the journey we've shared through these pages. The path through grief and loss is both profoundly personal and universally resonant. It is with a heart touched by both sorrow and hope that I offer these concluding words.

This book, crafted with a poetic literary grace, represents not just a recounting of my own experiences but a testament to the wider journey that many of us undertake. It is my sincere hope that these reflections, drawn from the depths of my own grief, will serve as a beacon of encouragement and inspiration. Through these words, I seek to share a message of surrender and solace—encouraging you to release your pain into the hands of God, trusting that His love and presence are steadfast even in our most troubled moments.

In the midst of our deepest sorrows, it is easy to feel isolated. To feel as though our cries are lost in a void. Yet, it is precisely in these moments of profound sadness that we are reminded of the unyielding love that surrounds us. The reality of grief can be overwhelming, but it is never without its counterpart in divine comfort. As I have navigated my own journey, I have been consistently reassured of the enduring truth that; although our connection with God may seem strained at times, it is never severed.

AFTERWORD

THIS BOOK STANDS AS A TESTAMENT

to that divine connection—a reminder that even when we are engulfed in the darkness of grief, we are enveloped in a love that transcends our understanding. To grieve deeply and authentically is not a sign of abandonment but an opportunity to experience a deeper embrace of God's unwavering compassion.

To all who have walked this journey with me through these pages, I offer my heartfelt thanks. Your willingness to engage with these intimate reflections has been a source of great strength. May you find in these words not just comfort but a renewed sense of connection to the divine presence that accompanies us through every trial.

As we conclude this shared journey, may we carry forward the knowledge that our most profound moments of pain are met with an equally profound capacity for healing and love. In every step of our grief, may we find courage and solace in the assurance that, even in our deepest sorrow, we are never alone.

AFTERWORD

THIS BOOK STANDS AS A TESTAMENT

to that divine connection—a reminder that even when we are engulfed in the darkness of grief, we are enveloped in a love that transcends our understanding. To grieve deeply and authentically is not a sign of abandonment but an opportunity to experience a deeper embrace of God's unwavering compassion.

To all who have walked this journey with me through these pages, I offer my heartfelt thanks. Your willingness to engage with these intimate reflections has been a source of great strength. May you find in these words not just comfort but a renewed sense of connection to the divine presence that accompanies us through every trial.

As we conclude this shared journey, may we carry forward the knowledge that our most profound moments of pain are met with an equally profound capacity for healing and love. In every step of our grief, may we find courage and solace in the assurance that, even in our deepest sorrow, we are never alone.

Printed in the USA
CPSIA information can be obtained
at www.ICGtesting.com
LVHW070902071224
798393LV00006B/61